796.8 Barnes, Ben E. *1237*
BAR
The beginner's guide
to better boxing

DATE		
SEP 1 5 1982 OCT 0 4 1996		
SEP 2 7 1982 DEC 0 7 2006		
OCT 3 1 APR 0 2 2007		
NOV 1 3 1983		
APR 4 1985		
OCT 1 8 1985		
DEC 4 1985		
MAR 2 9 1988		
MAY 1 7 1988		
SEP 2 0 1989		
APR 3 0 1993		

The Beginner's Guide to Better
BOXING

The Beginner's Guide to Better
BOXING

Ben E. Barnes and Kathlyn Gay

Foreword by Thomas L. "Sarge" Johnson
U.S.A. Boxing Coach, AMSPEC, U.S. State Department

Photographs by Douglas Gay

David McKay Company, Inc.
New York

Library of Congress Cataloging in Publication Data

Barnes, Ben E
  The beginner's guide to better boxing.

  Includes index.
  SUMMARY: An illustrated guide to boxing, including
equipment, conditioning, basic forms, blows,
defenses, rules, injuries, and style.
    1. Boxing—Juvenile literature. [1. Boxing]
I. Gay, Kathlyn, joint author. II. Gay, Douglas.
III. Title.

GV1136.B37   796.8'3   79-3451
ISBN 0-679-20533-0

    3 4 5 6 7 8 9 10
Manufactured in the United States of America

Contents

Acknowledgments

The authors acknowledge with deep appreciation the assistance and advice of Thomas L. "Sarge" Johnson, well known in amateur boxing circles as a "coaches' coach," who has spent many long hours coaching Olympic boxing teams and other international contenders. Mr. Johnson has also provided his own coaching manuals for our reference. His advice to prospective amateur boxers appears in the Foreword to this book. In addition, we would like to thank the members of an amateur boxing club in Elkhart, Indiana, who posed for photos and demonstrated some of the basic techniques of the boxing game.

—Ben E. Barnes and Kathlyn Gay

Foreword

Boxing is no ordinary game, as you will soon discover when reading the instructions and advice in this book. You may already be an accomplished athlete and have exceptional natural ability, but to be effective in boxing—or any other sport—you must learn the basic skills in their proper sequence. Along with acquiring skills comes the opportunity to develop confidence, willpower, and courage.

After coaching countless young men in the sport, including members of the 1976 U.S. Olympic boxing team in Montreal, Canada, I can point out dozens of ways that boxing benefits its participants. History, too, has shown us that the sport opens doors for many disadvantaged individuals in the United States. By winning world championships, a number of boxers in the professional arena have gone from poverty to prosperity and from obscurity to prominence. Among the well-known names from times past are: Jack Johnson, Jack Dempsey, Joe Louis, Rocky Marciano, and Joe Frazier—just a few who came up the hard way.

In amateur boxing, U.S. Olympic gold-medal winners Howard Davis, "Sugar" Ray Leonard, Leo Randolph, and the brothers Michael and Leon Spinks who rose to places in the spotlight within just a few short years. Several are now in the professional ranks, earning hundreds of thousands of dollars annually.

Fame and fortune aren't the only rewards of the sport. Whether amateur or professional, boxing teaches you how to accept criticism, how to turn hostility into an accepted form of behavior, and how to be humble as well as appreciate one's own worth. You learn to be patient and to have faith in yourself and in others. And through the sport, you will find friendship, encouragement, and approval.

Boxing also provides exceptional opportunities to develop and maintain physical endurance, agility, and coordination of hands and feet. You receive excellent training as a basis for physical fitness and mental alertness. You will learn complete body control and develop the skills of balance and fast, reflex action. You will use all parts of your body in more different planes and angles than you would in almost any other sport. As a boxer, you will have a chance to express your personality as you might in art forms such as music, dance or drama.

The sport is popular all over the world, as I can attest from traveling with boxing teams for international competitions and from presenting boxing programs and clinics—at the request of our State Department—in Indonesia, Japan, and several African nations. Boxing is one of the sports that helps to improve and cement our relationships with other peoples of the world.

It has been my privilege to serve as a good will ambassador through the sport of boxing and the U.S. State Department's International Communication Agency from 1974 through the present time. That total experience, plus my thirty years as an amateur boxing coach, have convinced me there is no better way to become a disciplined, productive, and healthy individual.

Thomas L. "Sarge" Johnson
U.S.A. Boxing Coach
AMSPEC U.S. State Department

Just as this book was ready to go to press, we heard about the tragic plane crash in Poland that took the lives of Mr. Johnson and a U.S. boxing team. With deepest sympathy to Mr. Johnson's family, we hope this book will carry on what he stood for and inspire young people to excel as "Sarge" would have exhorted them to do.

—Ben E. Barnes and Kathlyn Gay

Introduction

No one knows when the first two men raised their fists to fight in a contest and determine a winner. But historians believe boxing is one of the oldest forms of competition known to man.

Two thousand years ago, when professional gladiators entertained multitudes in the arenas of ancient Rome and Greece, boxing often meant fighting until the death of one of the opponents. Men wore leather straps, wrapped around their knuckles, wrists, and forearms. Called a *cestus* (ses-tus), the leather device was knotted or studded with brass spikes at the knuckles.

Over the centuries, boxing has changed, of course. Rules were established and referees were assigned to enforce them. But even in recent history, boxers have gone into the ring to fight to the finish—that is, they fought until one of the boxers was knocked out. Usually the fighters or pugilists (from the Latin word, *pugil,* meaning boxer) fought for money. This practice began in England over 200 years ago, when groups of men put a sum of money together as a "purse," or prize, then advertised for fighters to compete for it. Thus, the term "prizefighting" was born.

English and American prizefighters fought with bare knuckles until the now famous Queensberry rules were established. A wealthy English nobleman, the Marquis of Queensberry, who supported many prizefights, introduced the rules in 1865. These became the basis for the rules of the game today. Bare fists were outlawed. Gloves and a limited number of three-minute rounds were required. No thumb-gouging in the eye and no wrestling were permitted. The code also introduced the ten-count after a fighter had been knocked down. If the fighter could not rise after ten seconds—the count of ten—the fight was over and the floored fighter lost the bout.

Professional fighting in the United States today is governed by state laws. Codes vary from state to state, but the principal rules for the three-minute round, for the duties of officials, and for knockouts and fouls are generally the same. The professional game has created a great deal of excitement over the years, and heavyweight champions like Jack Dempsey, Gene Tunney, Joe Louis, Rocky Marciano, Joe Frazier, and Muhammad Ali have become more famous throughout the world than many presidents and kings.

In the amateur field, it is a different kind of game. Although some amateur boxers become well known because they win championships in Olympic Games and because many bouts are now televised, any boxer who accepts money for a fight would be barred from amateur competition. Also, the rules regarding the safety of both contenders in the ring are far more strict than in professional boxing.

Amateur boxing is governed by the Amateur Athletic Union of the United States (A.A.U.) and organizations like the Golden Gloves Association of America, and the National Collegiate Boxing Association. The sport no longer resembles anything like the violence, brutality, and gore that marked the ancient games.

Much to the surprise of many who oppose the game, the injury rate in amateur boxing shows that it is probably safer than other contact sports, such as football, basketball, and soccer. In a recent nationwide survey, amateur boxers who fought under A.A.U. rules had fewer injuries than other athletes, including those in track and field. The injury rate for high-school football, for example, is at least 46 percent. This means nearly half of all football players in high school receive injuries, most of which are serious or will bother the players throughout their lives. In contrast, amateur boxing injuries are less than 2 percent. Many of those injuries, like a bloody nose, would not even be recorded in other contact sports.

As you read about the basic techniques of boxing, you are really preparing yourself to learn under the guidance of a coach or trainer. No boxer can learn to box on his own. You need a partner or an opponent, of course, or there is no boxing match. But long before that point, you need a trained person to watch your moves, to show you your mistakes, and to help you improve.

This book will explain some of the first steps in learning the game and some rules of the ring. You will also find out what kind of equipment to buy to protect yourself and the safety of your opponent. Remember: *Safety is foremost.*

That in no way diminishes the excitement of the sport—or the challenge. A boxer keeps trying, again and again, to be the winner whenever he is matched with an opponent in the ring. He is not trying to prove he is a superman or to knock out every contender. Instead, he recognizes that boxing is a game of skills, and he wants to use those skills to better his own game.

The Beginner's Guide to Better
BOXING

1
Getting the Equipment

Boxing gloves are the most familiar pieces of equipment and often the first things you think about when you begin to box. At preschool age, you might have received a pair of play gloves as a gift. Now, you might own some inexpensive training gloves and use them to trade punches with your father, brother, or a friend. Or perhaps you use bag gloves on a regular basis to hit a speed bag for fun. But when you decide to train seriously and to learn the skills of boxing, you should also seriously consider the equipment you will need. The gloves will no longer be play things. The proper gloves are designed to protect your fists—and your opponent—from permanent injuries.

There are several types of boxing gloves. You will need *bag gloves* when you first practice throwing punches. These are used on a heavy training bag or on the smaller, speed (or striking) bag. Bag gloves look like heavy mittens with elastic at the wrists, and they are made of leather, with foam padding across the knuckles. There is a metal-weighted palm grip on the inside of a professional quality glove. Less expensive, youth bag gloves are designed with palm grips of foam or other padding material. The grip is just what the name implies—it helps you form a better grip, securing the position of your fingers in your palm. It also helps strengthen the palm and the fist itself.

Training gloves are made with much more padding than bag gloves. With their rounded curved styling over the hand and thumb, they look like small, leather-covered pillows. In fact, trainers refer to them as "pillow gloves" of various weights—12-ounce, 14-ounce, and 16-ounce. The extra weight is in the padding—a safety feature when boxers are practicing blows and blocks. You will need help to put on the gloves and to lace them tightly but comfortably. The ends of the laces must be wrapped around the cuffs of the gloves and tied securely at the back of the wrists so they won't dangle.

If you buy your own training or bag gloves, look for good quality. As a beginner in training, you don't need official A.A.U. boxing gloves, top pro gloves, or those designed for Golden Gloves competition. But the gloves should be well made and reinforced to take continual use. If you do not plan to practice on a regular basis, then a less expensive pair might do for an occasional or weekly workout. But poorly made gloves do not last, so it is best to pay a little more for quality and durability. That is a good rule to follow for any of your

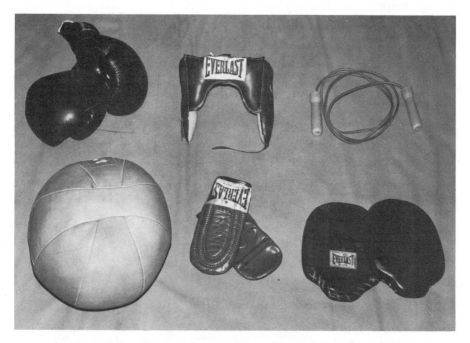

Some of the basic pieces of equipment for training in boxing skills are shown here. The pillow gloves (top left) are used when practicing blows and blocks with a partner. Next is a training headgear. The skip rope is used for conditioning, as is the medicine ball (lower left). The bag gloves are in the center, and the punch mitts (right) are held by a trainer while a boxer jabs at them.

boxing equipment, which you can buy in sporting goods stores or directly from companies that specialize in such products.

Once you have your own gloves, give them the best of care. Keep them clean, soft, and pliable with saddle soap. Hang them by their laces on a hook when you store them. Don't drop them on the floor or use them when they're dirty because you can cause injury or infection to yourself or your boxing partner if dirt from your gloves gets into an eye or an open cut.

You do not buy or use your own gloves for competition. They are furnished by the club or organization sponsoring a tournament. In amateur bouts sanctioned by A.A.U. 10-ounce boxing gloves are required for all classes of fighters. The gloves must also meet other A.A.U. requirements in their construction (such as the type of material used for padding), in the type and color of leather of the covering, and even in the type of label that is used to show A.A.U. approval. All of the regulations for competition gloves are intended to protect boxers from injuries that can easily occur when improper gloves are used.

Before you put on a pair of boxing gloves, you should wrap your hands with bandage material. This is one more protective measure. The wraps cover the knuckles and guard against bruises and scraped skin. They also support the wrists and prevent twisting and spraining. Hand wraps, made of cloth or elastic, are washable, and they should be washed regularly as a good health practice.

Disposable gauze bandages are used in competition, and the wrappings must be inspected before gloves are issued to a boxer. Instructions for wrapping the hands for practice or for competition are given in a later chapter.

There are two types of *head guards* that most boxers use. One is a *training headgear.* It, too, is padded and leather-covered to protect the head, temples, ears, and jaw. Some are made with cheek protectors. Even though *competition headgear* is optional for an amateur contest under A.A.U. rules, many district A.A.U. associations require headgear for bouts. Some coaches refuse to let their boxers compete without the competitive headgear because it provides added protection for all areas of the head. This kind of headgear must also meet rigid requirements for padding that will absorb the shock of blows.

An absolute must for A.A.U. competition fighting is a *mouthpiece.* Many coaches expect trainees to use a mouthpiece in practice also. Probably the least expensive of all your gear, this single mouthpiece of vinyl is used to protect the upper or lower teeth. The double mouthpiece covers both upper and lower teeth and gums, and it, too, is inexpensive.

You cannot fight in amateur competition without a *protective cup,* and it is a good policy to use one in practice as well. One type fits into an athletic supporter, and is designed to prevent injury when a boxer is hit below the belt. Another foul-proof cup is on a belt with padding, for hip and kidney protection.

Other types of wearing apparel you will need include: boxing trunks, shirt, athletic socks, and shoes. You can buy ten-inch-high boxing shoes of man-made leather. The genuine leather variety is usually twice as

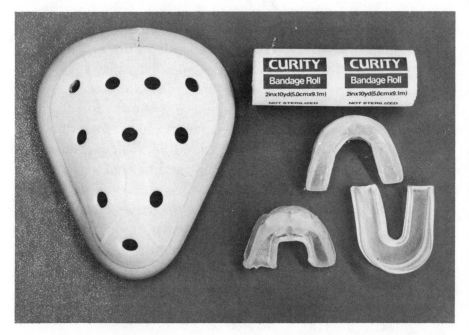

This type of protection cup (left) fits inside an athletic supporter. The bandages are the type used to wrap the hands for competition bouts. The vinyl mouthpieces can be softened in hot water, then shaped to fit the mouth.

costly. Boxing shoes are not required for competition (you can use regular athletic shoes or tennis shoes), but some boxers prefer them because the suction cups on the soles prevent sliding out of control in the ring. There cannot be any heels on shoes, and spikes and cleats are prohibited.

Most boxers do not own the full line of equipment for training that you would find in a boxing gym. A pear-shaped striking bag, or speed bag, is a familiar piece of equipment. It hangs from a swivel on a round platform, and a boxer practices punching the bag in continuous movements as it rebounds quickly. This helps to develop rhythm and speed. Because you work on a speed bag with arms raised, it also helps you develop the muscles in your upper arms. One word of caution: You cannot hit a speed bag in the same way that you should deliver blows, so do not expect to develop proper timing in this way.

You should practice a routine of blows on the training bag, usually called the heavy bag. It can weigh anywhere from 25 pounds for the junior size to 80 pounds for the champion leather bag. Canvas bags, found in most gyms, are lined with nylon and foam and are stuffed with a filler. You use the heavy bag to practice blows before you spar with another boxer in a ring. The bag also helps you to develop power and form.

Many young boxers start out with homemade bags. You can make one with a canvas duffel bag. Stuff it with thick, firm foam or a combination of sawdust, sand, and foam. The bag should be plump and firm when full. Tie it at the top and hang it from a hook.

The heavy bag is a basic piece of equipment, found in a boxing gym. Here, a coach is instructing a boxer on the proper form for a left jab, which he will practice on the heavy bag.

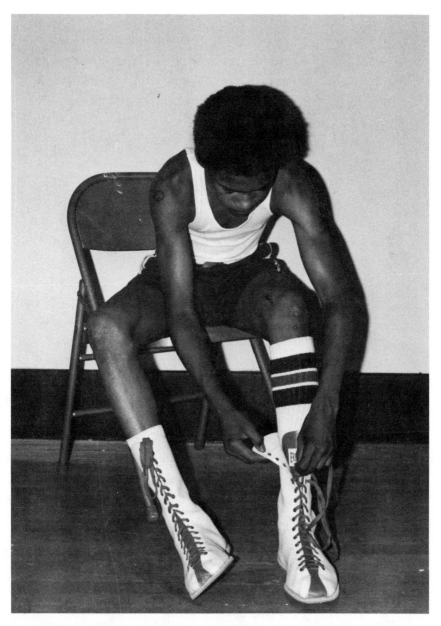

A boxer laces up a pair of boxing shoes, which are not required for competition, but provide support for the ankles when boxing.

While these bags do not last long, they are inexpensive and easy to remake.

Another piece of equipment that can be used at home is the skip rope. There are a variety of lengths, and you should be able to find one to fit your size—or simply cut a length of rope for that purpose. The rope is an important part of the conditioning explained in the next chapter.

In a boxing gym, you will probably be introduced to a leather-covered medicine ball that weighs from 5 to 15 pounds. A coach or trainer can help you use it to tone your stomach muscles. You lie on your back and tighten your stomach muscles as the ball is dropped a short distance on your stomach. Or you can work with a partner who holds the ball at waist level, pushing it out, so you can catch it in your midsection. You return the ball in the same way.

At home, you can get the same conditioning effect with an old spare tire. Let a partner bounce the tire on your stomach, just as the medicine ball would be used.

In almost every boxing gym you will see full-length mirrors. You can shadowbox—practice delivering blows—in front of the mirror. This is a good way to check that you are learning the proper form.

Competition boxing rings are very expensive, so you won't find a standard ring in most gyms. In competition, a ring is on an elevated platform, and there are regulations for such things as padding, size, and the type of floor that may be used. But many coaches, and boxers who train at home, mark off a ring area or set up a floor-level ring to substitute for the official type. The standard ring is about 20 feet square, with padded

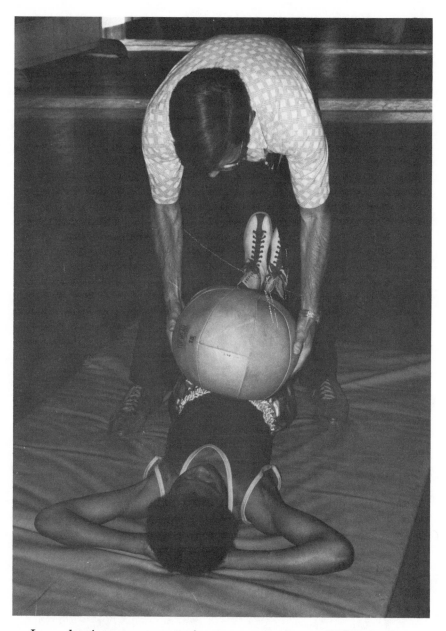

In a boxing gym, a trainer can use a medicine ball, dropping it a short distance on your stomach to help you tone your muscles.

corner posts for safety. Three ropes extend around the square ring, an equal distance apart.

Whether you have your own boxing equipment or use the equipment in a gym, protect it just as you want to be protected from abuse. Gym equipment is expensive, as is the minimum amount of boxing gear for one person. The equipment will last a long time if you maintain it.

Some general rules:

Keep your mouthpiece clean. Wash it in very hot water and store it in a plastic bag.

Have several pairs of hand wraps. Fold them neatly after use and wash them weekly.

Wash your gym clothes regularly. Don't roll them up and stuff them into a gym bag day after day, week after week.

Air your gloves and shoes.

Keep leather goods soft with the proper kinds of oils.

Don't use gloves or a medicine ball on rough surfaces.

Use the heavy bag for boxing practice. Don't kick, tackle or swing on it.

Use all equipment as it was designed to be used. Each piece of equipment is only as good as the person who uses and cares for it.

2
Conditioning

Now that you have learned about the equipment, you may think you are ready to box. But conditioning comes first. All athletes must prepare their bodies, developing strength and coordination. However, in boxing, unlike team sports, you have to depend solely on yourself in the ring; there is no teammate to help you; it's you against the opponent. The two of you might be evenly matched in skills and experience, but the boxer in the best physical and mental condition will most likely be the winner.

Physical and mental conditioning can hardly be separated in boxing. As you begin to develop the strength, speed, power, coordination, and stamina to box, you are also beginning to discipline your mind. There is no easy way to train, and you must create a routine for proper training. This in turn helps you create an attitude of dedication. You set your mind to build, to constantly maintain your body—because that is really all you have to work with. The gloves and other equipment are merely extensions of yourself.

If you begin your conditioning routine at home, start with at least a half hour of calisthenics every day. *Plan to get tired.* The exercises will be of little benefit if you are not truly working your body and, once again, setting your mind. Determine to continue, even though you might be uncomfortable.

You have probably learned a number of body-building exercises in gym classes at school, but here is a routine that works well with young boxers:

1. Perform 100 jumping jacks, then 100 sit-ups. You'll find that you can easily do 40 or 50 of each, so you can build up to 100 repetitions in only a week's time—*if* you cannot perform the total number on your first try.

2. Do 10 push-ups, then stand and run in place for one minute. Do 10 more push-ups, stand, and run in place. Repeat until you can do 50 push-ups.

3. For a leg-raise exercise, lie flat on your back and raise your legs about ten inches off the floor. Hold the position, spread your legs apart, then bring them together again. While your legs are raised parallel to the floor, pound on your stomach with your fists in a steady rhythm. Lower your legs to the floor. Repeat until you can do this routine 30 times.

4. Do the bicycle. Lie flat on your back, with your hands under your hips, raising your buttocks off the floor, legs up, rotating them like you are riding a bicycle. Continue for one minute.

14

Push-ups are a good conditioning exercise.

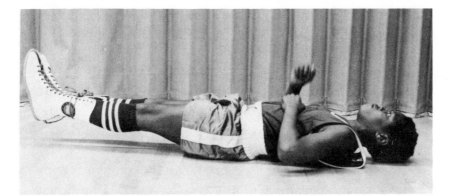

As part of a leg-raise exercise, pound on your stomach with your fists while your legs are raised parallel to the floor.

5. With your hands on your hips, drop onto your heels in a squat. Stand and squat again, repeating up to 100 times. Then "duck-walk" in a squatting position for 30 seconds.

6. Raise your arms on each side of your head, fingers almost touching the ears, and palms out. Stretch back until your arms quiver, and hold for the count of ten. Repeat ten times.

7. Use the skip rope for four rounds. In amateur boxing, a round can be one to three minutes in length, depending on the age and weight division of the fighter. (The divisions are explained in Chapter 6.) Skip with the rope for a round suitable for your age and weight, rest, then repeat three more times. Skipping rope (not jumping) is an ideal way for a boxer or any athlete to exercise. All of your body is in motion, and skipping helps you develop rhythm and timing. It is also an excellent conditioner for your feet, ankles, and legs.

8. If you can go to a boxing gym that has wall pulleys, you can warm up with these, getting loose and relaxed for the rest of the workout. The pulleys also help you strengthen your shoulder, back, and arm muscles. You can face the pulleys or work with your back to them. Keep your chin down as you exercise, and work in a smooth, fast pattern. Do not jerk the weights.

9. Weight lifting should *not* be included in your conditioning program. Bulging muscles will slow down your reflexes. You can use small hand weights or wear wrist and ankle weights for strengthening purposes.

10. *Roadwork is a must for conditioning.* If there is no time for anything else, take time to run. You do not

have to jog for several miles. Instead, do *wind sprints*. This means you run at top speed for one hundred yards, then walk for a hundred yards. Repeat this procedure until you have gone a mile. Another method is to run the length of time you would box in a round, walk for a minute, then run another round, repeating for three rounds.

Running will help you build wind, strengthening your lungs and heart, as well as your legs. You should run every day when you start to train. After you build endurance and and are able to run without huffing and puffing, you can taper off, running three or four times a week. The important thing to remember is that roadwork is a way to develop stamina. You will need that staying power in the ring.

Many other athletes, such as weight lifters, karate experts, and wrestlers, try to match themselves with boxers, believing their muscular strength alone is enough to overpower boxers. But they will not last even one round if they have not developed the kind of stamina needed to keep their arms swinging. The total conditioning routine of a boxer should be toward that end. To repeat, a well-conditioned boxer can emerge a winner over another boxer of equal or even superior skill if the other boxer is not in good physical shape and cannot endure.

When you go to a boxing gym, a coach will have his own routine for calisthenics and roadwork—one which he will expect you to follow. Most of the routines just mentioned will probably be included, but there will be additional mental conditioning. You will learn to listen.

A good coach constantly talks to a boxer, telling

him how to improve and reminding him to think, think, think about what he is doing. Amateur boxing is *not* brute force; it is more like a chess game in which you are trying to outwit your opponent. You should learn to use your mind, as well as your hands, to box.

You should also develop confidence in yourself. This will take the help of a coach and some experience in the ring with other boxers. But you can begin by talking to yourself. If you are tired or get hurt while boxing, try not to show it. Tell yourself that the other boxer is just as tired and feels just as bad as you do. Don't forget an opponent has just been through the same exchange of blows. Although this part of the mental conditioning isn't easy, it goes along with the physical buildup.

Some of the psychology of Muhammad Ali can apply here. Ali not only tells himself but he lets the whole world know that he believes he is "the greatest." In the ring he never let the other boxer know if he had been hurt. Instead, he would taunt and urge the opponents on, which sometimes helped defeat boxers who became confused or upset by these tactics.

The flamboyant Ali may have clowned in front of TV and news cameras, but there is no doubt that his conditioning was a serious matter. There is also little doubt that Ali has always been a sharp, fast thinker in the ring. As only Ali could put it, after he regained the title from George Foreman in 1974: "The bull [meaning Foreman] is stronger, but the matador [Ali] is smarter."

The cool approach of an Ali is not just a mask. You should learn to be at ease, both in and out of training and while you are boxing. This is part of conditioning, too. If you have trouble resting or sleeping, read a good book, take a warm bath, listen to quiet music, or watch a funny movie. Sometimes the company of a good friend can help you unwind if you are tense before you box.

For relaxation and inspiration, it helps to read about the dedication and training methods of famous boxers of the past. The late Gene Tunney, for example, did not become a champion heavyweight fighter until later in his career, even though he was a natural at boxing. He had to use a lot of will power and mental conditioning to get himself to that point. One sportswriter said Tunney had weak and brittle hands. To strengthen them, Tunney carried two hard rubber balls in his pockets. He would squeeze them whenever he had a moment. He also exercised each finger by using it as a lever to push himself away from a wall. He repeated this 500 times for each finger every day!

The famous Jack Dempsey, who held the heavyweight championship title before Tunney, said he built up his punching power because of "a hard, steady grind for several years" on the heavy bag. He pointed out that many people did not realize how long and how hard he worked on the big bag. The point he made sixty years ago applies today. You have to repeat, repeat, repeat—practicing and perfecting your skills constantly. You cannot be an on-again, off-again trainee if you want to be skillful in the ring.

Other important parts of your conditioning program are diet and personal hygiene. Cleanliness and care of the outer body are important for any good health program. Shower after working out. Keep a clean towel in your gym bag. Take care of your feet. Make sure your shoes fit properly and that you have comfortable socks. Wear two pairs of socks if you need them to cushion your feet. Wear your boxing trunks slightly loose, but your shirt should fit snugly so the straps won't fall off your shoulders. Don't wear rings or other jewelry during training or in competition. They cause injuries.

Be smart about what you eat. What you put inside your body has a lot to do with your overall health and well-being. The strength that you need to box comes from nutritious food, meaning food your body can use to build and maintain body tissues and produce energy. A proper diet for any athlete includes: plenty of fresh fruit and vegetables; lean meat or fish that is broiled, baked, or roasted; dairy products, such as eggs, milk, and cheese; and whole-grain or enriched bread and cereals. An occasional soda and bag of chips won't destroy you, and candy, pop, and other snack foods are fun to eat and taste good. But *avoid these foods as much as you can.* Part of conditioning is learning how to discipline your eating habits along with establishing a regular routine for physical and mental exercise. Remember: *All parts of your body work together.* It's the only team a boxer has.

With that in mind, there is no point being a doper, drinker, or smoker. Drugs, alcohol, and cigarettes do not build the body. They destroy it.

If you establish good health habits early in your conditioning program, your training routine will be a lot easier to follow. Most amateur boxing programs are not seasonal, so your conditioning can be year round. That means you will have concentrated training sessions before a competition, and at other times you will be working out to keep yourself in shape. Conditioning, then, is more than training to survive in the ring. It's a way of life.

3
The Basic Forms

The Fist

WARNING: A fist that is incorrectly formed can lead to broken fingers or other hand injuries. This section begins on a note of caution, because a beginning boxer often clenches the hand in the wrong way to make a fist.

When you form a fist, *do not* tuck your thumb inside your fingers like this:

Do not let your thumb poke out like this:

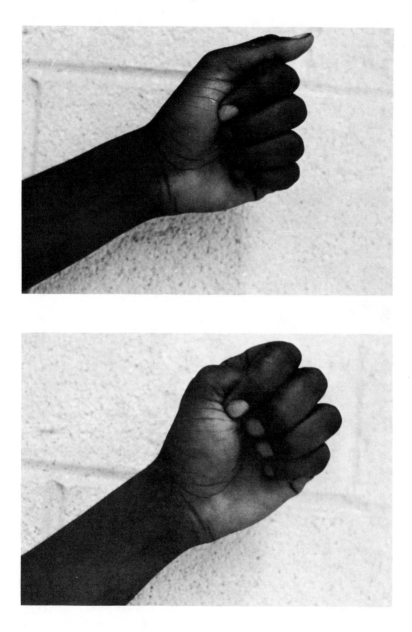

Do not twist your wrist or bend it like this

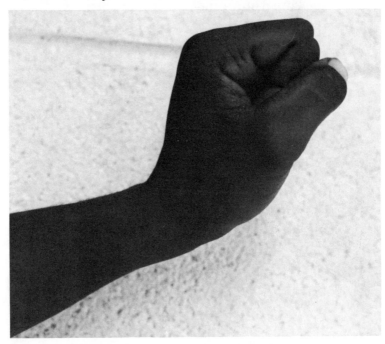

or drop it like this:

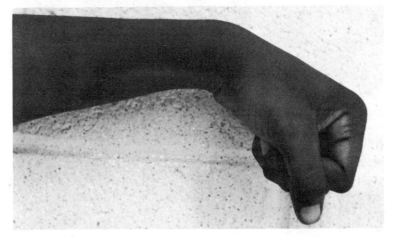

Form a tight fist by clenching your fingers into the palm of your hand. Fold your thumb across the fingers. You should have a flat surface on the thumb side of your hand, like this:

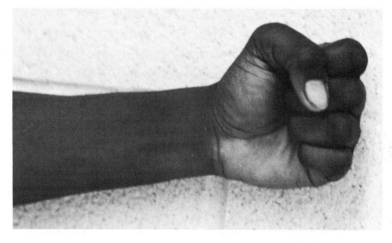

Now hold your arm and fist straight out in front of you. Keep your arm and wrist in a rigid line, with your fist in line with the wrist like this:

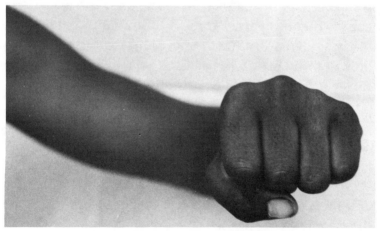

Think of your wrist and hand as one unit. Always keep your wrist rigid.

When a blow is delivered, your arm should drive directly out, aiming straight for your target. It should snap back in the same direct line, almost as if your arm were a piston in an engine. As your arm snaps out, your hand (with a firm wrist) should turn slightly so that the thumb side of your fist is inward and the knuckles are up for the impact. Then the large knuckles of your fist can take the shock as you deliver a blow.

The Stance

Even though it is very important to use your arm and fist correctly, the power of any punch must come from your body. An arm and fist simply carry the force that is created when you put the weight of your body behind them.

After you learn to form your fists correctly, stand in front of a mirror to practice the on-guard stance. This is the basic position for your feet, body, and arms. "On guard" means exactly that. A boxer should always be ready to defend against attack and ready to deliver a blow. From this basic position, you should be able to throw a punch or block your opponent's punch without losing your balance. Here's how:

First, stand with your feet apart at a slight angle. Then put your left foot forward as though you were going to walk in a natural stride.

(If you are left-handed, start with your right foot and proceed with the opposite side as you follow the directions.)

Next, shift your weight over your left foot. Let your right heel raise an inch or two off the floor. The left foot should stay nearly flat. Your left shoulder should be in line with your left foot, thus your left leg would form an angular line with the left side of your body. Think of your left side as a hinge. You will swing your body weight around it.

Now, bend your knees so that your legs feel springy, but your body well balanced. Swing your body from the waist, left then right. You should be comfortable and be able to maintain your balance without moving your feet. If not, change the position of your right foot. Move it out slightly if you need to widen your stance. Move it in toward your body if you need to narrow your stance.

With your feet in position, raise your fists, letting your elbows fold to the body, forming neat "check marks." The elbows should never tilt behind or out, like flapping wings. They should be positioned to protect your ribs and each side of your body.

Place your left fist about an inch higher than your shoulder and about eight to ten inches from your chin. Your right fist should be a few inches to the right

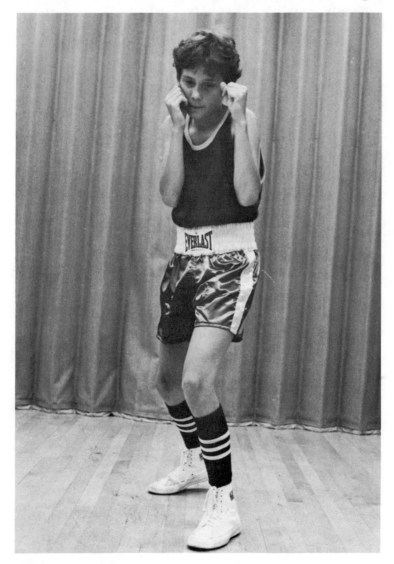

of your jaw, just below the ear. Tuck your chin toward your left shoulder and breast bone. If you do not keep your chin down, it becomes an easy target for your opponent.

As you take the on-guard position, your left shoulder and hip (the "hinge side" of your body) form a shield for protection. You also attack from this position, with your left fist up and ready to strike.

Practice the on-guard stance until you are able to take the position automatically. You should be able to take the stance just like a basketball player stands ready at the free-throw line or a baseball player takes a stance at bat. This basic stance must be mastered, since all moves start from the on-guard position and return to it.

In a gym, a coach will check to see that you are taking the stance correctly. At home, ask someone who is knowledgeable about boxing to check your form. Try to correct any bad habits early. It is hard to change if you use improper methods for a long time.

The Hand Wraps

Once you learn the basic form for your fists and the stance, you can wrap your hands and prepare for practice with the gloves. Use the plain cloth or elastic hand wraps with loops for the thumbs, as described in the first chapter. The gauze bandage is expensive for practice because it must be thrown away after one use.

Always wrap your hands before you put on gloves to practice. The little extra time it takes is time well spent because it will prevent injuries to your hands.

A coach or trainer can show you how to wrap your hands. There are variations on the basic bandaging technique, but the main purpose is to protect your knuckles and thumbs and to hold your wrists firm. Some trainers wrap hands by working in layers—from well back on each wrist toward the knuckles—with one or two layers around the thumb. Boxers with weak wrists want extra wrap to provide more strength. Some prefer a tighter wrap than others.

After you watch someone wrap your hands a few times, you will be able to do it yourself. You can use the directions that follow for a criss-cross method of hand wrapping:

First, put the loop of the hand wrap over your thumb. Take the wrap under your wrist and make one complete lap around the wrist. Bring the wrap across

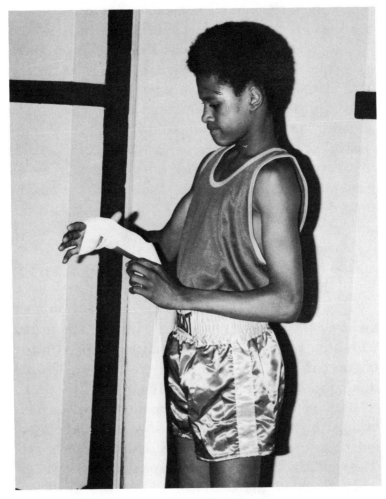

Take the wrap between the thumb and finger.

the top of the hand, in a diagonal, toward the thumb joint, taking it between the thumb and first finger. Lap the wrap under and over the knuckles. Lap once more.

Next, go under and cross over your thumb, pulling the thumb snugly—but not too tightly—to the hand, as you take the wrap under the knuckles. Lap the knuckles again to the base of the little finger. Bend the fingers to see if the wrap is fitting comfortably.

Cross over the top of the hand, in a diagonal, to the base of the thumb, then under the wrist. Now make one complete lap around the wrist. Then cross the top of the hand in a diagonal to the thumb joint, taking the wrap between the thumb and finger, then under and over the knuckles again. Make the diagonal from the base of the little finger, across the top of the hand, to the base of the thumb. If you have a short piece of wrap remaining, layer it around the wrist, working up toward the arm until you can tie it securely with the ties.

For small hands, there may be enough wrap left to lap the wrist, then make the third diagonal across the top of the hand to the thumb joint, bringing the wrap between the thumb and finger once more. Go under and over the knuckles to the base of the little finger. Now bring the wrap in the last diagonal across the top of the hand to the wrist. Lap the remaining wrap around the wrist and tie securely.

In competition, the hand wraps must be gauze bandaging. Only one ten-yard roll of gauze can be used, but there are more layers than with the cloth bandages and the wrap is laced between fingers as well as layered around the wrists and knuckles. You need more protection with the lighter-weight 10-ounce gloves used in competition. The heavier pillow gloves have the additional padding needed for practice.

Fundamental Footwork

In boxing, the basic footwork is called "shuffling." The feet barely leave the floor, and one foot follows after the other a short distance apart. You should glide forward and back, almost like dancing except that you *never* cross your legs or walk. All footwork should be done in quick but smooth steps in the on-guard position.

When you use the proper footwork, you move your body easily, keeping your balance, and you are always ready to attack and defend yourself. After you learn the footwork, you must coordinate it with the basic blows. The coordination of hands and feet is an art in itself. But first you must learn how to take the steps.

There are four basic moves—advancing (going forward), retreating (moving backward), circling left, and circling right. All footwork starts from and maintains the on-guard position. Assume that position for the *forward shuffle.* Your lead foot—the left foot—should slide forward about two inches. Then slide your right foot forward two inches. Continue to move forward in this same pattern, left foot sliding, right foot sliding after it. Always move each foot the same distance. Keep the on-guard position with the left foot nearly flat on the floor and the heel of the right foot raised slightly. Remember, the left shoulder should be in line with your left foot.

The boxer on the right is demonstrating how to circle left.

He slides the left foot to the left and brings up the right foot in the correct position.

Never cross your legs like this when boxing.

Now practice the *backward shuffle*. Once again, you are in the on-guard position. Move your right foot backward, then follow with the left. Keep the same distance and position of the feet and body as you did when moving forward. Slide your feet as you shuffle back. *Do not walk* backward.

Practice both the forward and backward shuffle. You can move along a line on the floor, always keeping your fists raised and your legs apart in the on-guard position. Don't forget to keep your knees loose with constant springlike movements. Also, remember to glide and slide. Move forward with the left foot and follow with the right. Go backward on the right foot, following with the left. Any time you have a chance, practice advancing and retreating so that these movements can be done without thinking about them.

When you circle in boxing, you make a diagonal movement, but you also move as though following a circular path around your opponent. To *circle left,* take the on-guard stance. Slide your left foot to the left about six inches. Then—remembering that your left side is like a hinge—pivot your body to the left and bring up the right foot in the correct position again. Continue circling in this manner, moving to the left with your lead foot and following with the right. Angle around until you form a complete circle.

To *circle to the right,* lead with the right foot but "push off" with the left. This should be a short, snappy movement. If you learn to move on the balls of your feet, you should be able to slide quickly out of the way of an opponent's punch. That is the point of circling—to make yourself a difficult target to hit.

4
The Basic Blows

Now you can begin to box, but remember that boxing is not a matter of just throwing punches in a haphazard way. It is a sport in which you are trying to outhit the other boxer. You must learn the art of hitting—a system of blows that requires timing and body power rather than just arm power. The weight of the body must be shifted so that the hip and shoulder move before the arm and fist land the blow.

Start with four basic *straight blows*. All straight blows are designed for speed because they travel less distance than hooks or swings, which arc out before striking. A straight blow is an arm's length away, which means you are more likely to hit your target.

The *left jab* is the most fundamental straight blow

in boxing, and it is the basis for other types of blows that follow. Start from the on-guard position. Strike out with the left fist in a straight line, using quick, rhythmic movements to your opponent's head or chin. Your fist should snap out, then back, just as swiftly, to the on-guard position. As your arm snaps out, you should keep the wrist firm, turning the fist slightly so that the knuckles are up when you strike, like this:

As you deliver the left jab, you should also be stepping forward with your left foot, pushing off with your right. Put the weight of your left shoulder into your blow.

Before you practice the left jab, you should know what it can do for you. It is both an offensive and defensive weapon. The left jab gives you an opportunity to hold your opponent out away from you, not let him get in close so that he can reach you with a punch. It is a "feeler" that helps you learn how your opponent is going to react to your punches and how he is going to defend himself. The blow is a way to use strategy in the game. You can set up your opponent. By keeping up a steady pattern of annoying, antagonizing jabs, you can throw him off balance. This will help you find openings for other blows with the right hand.

The left jab is not meant to be a power punch. Rather, it is the art of being able to deliver blows in rapid succession to worry another fighter, like a bee buzzing around his head. Ali's well-known phrase ". . . sting like a bee" refers to his jab, which was perfected to the point where he could keep up a constant barrage of stinging punches. Most famous boxers, whether professional or amateur, have used the left jab effectively. But it takes strength and stamina. A boxer has to be in good condition, otherwise his arm gets too tired to keep pecking, jarring, and stinging the opponent. At the same time, a boxer must get ready to hit with a more powerful right punch.

In order to develop the left jab, you must practice it over and over again. You can practice on the heavy bag, while shadowboxing and sparring (which you will learn about later), and in your mind. In other words, determine that you are going to create the best left jab you are capable of producing. Plan to spend time on it day after day. Think about the delivery when you are not actually practicing it. Be rhythmic. Find a "beat," a rat-a-tat-tat like a drum, that you can repeat to yourself or hear in your mind as you practice delivery. Two or three jabs at a time are not enough. You should practice six, eight, ten—as many as you can—one after the other.

The *straight right* is the basic blow that often follows a left jab once you have created an opening for it. If you have bothered your opponent enough so that he drops his arms and is not defending himself properly, you can deliver a power blow with the right fist. Once again, aim for the head with a straight blow from the shoulder. Your arm should not arc. Deliver the blow

The straight right is the basic blow that follows a left jab, once you have created an opening for it.

from the basic stance with a twist of your waist. Snap your right arm straight out.

The force of the straight right comes from the shift of body weight. Don't forget that the left side of your body is a hinge. It will seem natural to swing your whole right side forward on that hinge, shifting your weight from your right to the left leg. Keep your right foot on the floor. Just as your fist connects with its target, your right arm should be extended.

If you have natural power in your right, practice developing it so that the blow can be delivered swiftly. Some fighters have been able to perfect such a fast delivery that it is hard to see it when thrown.

A devastating right hand has made many professional boxers famous. In 1959, Ingemar Johansson of Sweden won the heavyweight championship from Floyd Patterson because of what sportswriters called his "stunning right hand." One reporter said, "Ingo's right flipper did more damage than a crane with an iron ball on the end of it." In earlier years, Jack Dempsey, Joe Louis, and Rocky Marciano were just a few of the world boxing champions to stagger and knock out contenders with what Marciano called a "Suzie-Q"—a dynamite right.

The *left to the body* is a blow delivered like the jab to the head. Starting from the on-guard position, step forward with your left foot and push off with your right. Use quick rhythmic movements, but this time aim for your opponent's midsection. The purpose of this blow is to force your opponent to drop his guard as he tries to protect himself from body punches. You

want to create an opening so that your opponent's head or chin is a clear target.

While you are delivering the left to the body, your arm does not arc. Snap the left arm straight out, but stretch a little more than you would with the left jab to the head. Your knees should bend slightly, as though you are going into a crouch. Protect your chin from your opponent's blows by keeping it down and behind your left shoulder. Keep an open right hand in front of your chin as a guard.

The *right to the body* is also a snappy blow delivered straight from the shoulder.

This can be a forceful blow and it, too, is used to bring your opponent's guard down. It can be effective after you have thrown several left jabs, flicking them out to annoy your opponent.

When you deliver the right to the body, start as with all blows from the on-guard position. Drop into a semi-crouch, reach and throw the straight right to the body, then snap back into the on-guard position.

The *left hook* is one more basic blow, but it can be the most difficult for a beginner to master. It should be taught after you have reached the intermediate or advanced level. But you need to know what a left hook is and how to use it.

The blow is both an offensive and defensive weapon. It is most often used to counter-punch, which is a blow that will offset and defend against a punch delivered by an opponent. As you deliver a left hook, arc your left arm toward the head. Never allow your arm to swing wide. The blow is short, hardly more than six to eight inches. It carries a lot of power because your entire body is behind it. You should deliver it from the basic position, but do not move forward on your left foot. Instead, pivot so that the left side of your body swings into the punch. Complete the pivot just as your fist hits its target, as shown.

Sometimes the hook is aimed at the body, but such a blow could technically be called an *uppercut*. This is also a short blow. You can deliver a left or right uppercut, but the left is most often used by the less experienced boxer who should always keep the right hand on guard for protection.

Start from the basic position, but get ready to drop your left. Your fist should drop below your opponent's midsection, which is your target. Keep the right hand up, in position. Bend your knees as if you are going to crouch slightly. Then shoot your fist up, while pivoting on your left foot and straightening your legs. The three actions should happen at the same time: Shoot, pivot, straighten. This is what creates the power of the blow.

You will need coaching help to learn and to practice the uppercut and left hook. But you can practice the basic straight blows on your own in several different ways. First, learn to *shadowbox*. This means that you practice the delivery of blows, one at a time or in combination, against an imaginary opponent. You pretend to punch a shadow. This is an important part of practice because you deliver the blows in the correct form, learning the feel and movements for each one. Practice each blow for at least three rounds. Then shadowbox in front of a full-length mirror to check your form and delivery.

Shadowbox in front of a full-length mirror to check your form and delivery.

As you shadowbox, practice breath control, too. Breathe in a steady rhythm, exhaling through the nostrils in snorts. This may not seem proper in polite company, but quick exhales or snorts help you coordinate your breathing with the snap of your fist. Incorrect breathing can cause you to tire easily and become winded.

You should also practice basic blows on the heavy bag. If you do not have one at home, try to find a gym where boxing equipment is available. Practice each blow on the heavy bag for three rounds, working for power and rhythm. Because the heavy bag resists the impact of your blow, you learn to snap your punch, to pull back into position quickly before the bag swings into you. Practice leaning into and away from the bag, learning to sway from the waist without changing your position or to pivot left and right.

After three or four weeks of work on the heavy bag, along with shadowboxing, you will be able to practice with a real partner in the ring. This *sparring* practice, as it is called, should be done under the supervision of a qualified coach. Usually, you will start your sparring practice with an experienced boxer who can "catch" your punches, acting like a "dummy" or another punching bag. This way you can learn how it feels to throw punches and hit an opponent. (At the same time, your partner is practicing defensive techniques.)

When you begin to box in the ring with a partner, you will probably throw a combination of punches without realizing it. Beginners often pound away, flailing one fist after the other at an opponent—with no real plan in mind. You cannot box without combination punches. However, you will soon learn that *combination-punching* is a precise method of delivering blows in a pattern. It is an offensive technique to break through your opponent's guards and blocks.

After you have learned the basic left jab, straight right, and left hook, you can put these blows together and practice combination punches. Some coaches teach combinations by the number system. The left jab is called basic punch number one, the straight right is number two, and the left hook is number three. The basic combination punch is the left jab and straight right in sequence, so it follows that the basic combination would be called the "one-two."

To deliver this sequence, take the basic position. Step forward on the left foot and jab with the left fist. Slide your right foot forward and deliver the straight right. Make sure that your right arm is completely extended. As soon as you complete the one-two combination, snap back to the on-guard position, ready to deliver other blows or to block punches from your opponent.

The one-two is the basis for all other combination punches, so you should try to perfect it before you move on to other sequences. Practice on a heavy bag; in front of the mirror, shadowboxing; and with a sparring partner in the ring. As you deliver the left jab followed by the straight right, rhythm and speed are very important. If you have ever watched Muhammad Ali in action, you have seen the one-two mastered to perfection. His speed in delivering this combination is what helped to make it so successful. It has often been said that Ali could punch faster than you could blink your eye.

The next combination to practice is the one-two-three. When you deliver this pattern, add the left hook to the one-two combination as shown.

If you can put two combinations together during your beginning stages as a boxer, you will be doing very well. Once again, it takes practice—and more practice. Everyone develops at a different pace, so you might advance very quickly to other combinations. Possibly you will learn the one-three combination, which is the same as saying the left jab–left hook. This pattern is a fairly simple one *if* you have learned to throw the basic jab and hook correctly.

As usual, start from the on-guard position. Never drop your right as you deliver the blows with the left. After you jab, pull back quickly and whip a left hook to the head while pivoting on your left foot. The actions should be so swift that they seem to be happening all at once. That's the secret of any effective combination punch.

You can add the straight right to the one-three combination for the one-three-two pattern, or you might create your own combinations as you progress in your boxing skills. The advantage of using combinations is that it creates an element of surprise when you box. Your opponent will not always know what to expect and can become confused by different patterns.

Remember that any combination is made up of *basic blows,* which should be practiced regularly as

Jab with the left, as demonstrated here, to set up for the right as shown below.

Finish the 1-2-3 combination with a left hook.

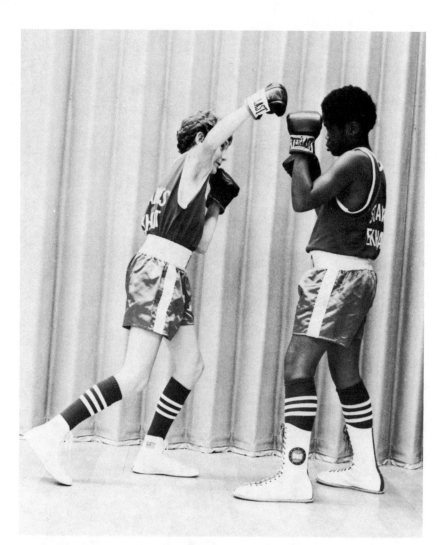

Don't use a roundhouse blow as demonstrated here.
When you swing wide like this, you leave yourself open for
blows from your opponent.

part of your workout routine. While practicing, keep these tips in mind:

1. Never use a "round-house" blow, which is a swing in a wide circle. It takes longer to reach the target, and a wide swing will not protect you the way a straight punch will.

2. Always follow through with your punch. Don't "shorten up" and lose your power.

3. Punch through your opponent's defense or guard; don't punch at it.

4. Don't push your blow. Snap your punch and hit hard.

5. Punch with a purpose as soon as you see an opening. Don't wait to be punched.

6. Keep your wrist rigid, but rotate your fist about a quarter of a turn as you deliver a blow.

7. Don't lean back. Step in to hit.

8. Never drop your guard. When one fist is delivering a blow, the other should be up in a protective position. Keep your hands high when you are not delivering a blow.

5
Basic Defenses

You already know that to be on guard is one way to defend yourself against blows. The on-guard position also illustrates that the hands, forearms, elbows, and shoulders can be protective shields, blocking blows as they come toward you.

In boxing, you will constantly shift from attack to defense, so you need to learn a variety of ways to block, guard, duck, and parry. These strategies are as important as hitting properly. For your own safety, you must know how to protect yourself.

Just as you want to outhit your opponent, so you should try to outwit him in defensive measures. That is one of the basic techniques—to think far enough ahead so you know what your opponent is going to do next and can be prepared. This takes experience in the ring. While you are gaining that experience, you can study and practice some basic defensive methods.

The *catch* is a block with an open glove, and it is usually used against a left jab. Hold your arm up with your palm toward the opponent. Catch a blow in your glove as you would catch a baseball. Your wrist should be rigid as the blow strikes.

A skillful boxer can catch blows as easily as picking apples off a tree. The ease comes because he has learned to absorb the force of the blow in a relaxed manner, letting the blow come to him, not reaching out for it.

Another fundamental block is with the *back of the right glove* to protect against a left hook to the head.

The *shoulder block* is used against the straight right. Turn your body slightly to the right so that you catch the blow on your left shoulder muscle.

The *elbow block* is used in a similar way against

With the elbow block, the elbow and forearm are used as a shield against a body blow.

right-hand blows, except that the elbow acts as the shield. Remember also that in the proper on-guard position, the elbows are pinned against the body to protect your sides and ribs from blows.

Ducking is a natural defense. You instinctively duck when an object comes flying at you, and it is a good form of defense when blows are hooking or swinging toward your head. However, you do not just drop your head or crouch. Instead, keep your guard up, step in toward your opponent, and bend your knees, leaning forward at the waist. One precaution: Be very careful about ducking below your opponent's belt line, which is a foul. In competition, you could receive a scoring penalty.

The *parry* is a means of defense used to push aside or brush away a blow. There are many different ways to

Use an arm and glove movement to parry a blow.

parry, depending on the type of blow you are defending against. But you always use an arm and glove movement. Your elbows should stay in close to the body to protect your ribs and sides. Then the forearm works from the elbow, moving from either side to brush an oncoming blow inward or outside. You can also parry a blow up or down, actually changing the direction or path of a punch with very quick but precise movements. For example, if your opponent delivers a left jab, use an inside parry, which means your right hand would be on the inside of the oncoming blow. The palm of your right hand would be outward as you brush the jab away to the outside.

A *clinch* is easily recognized by anyone who watches boxing. It is simply holding your opponent's arms so he is unable to hit you. You move in quickly on your opponent and pin his arms to the sides of your body by holding them under your arms. You actually entwine his arms, working them up under your armpits. This is a defensive move to gain time if you are tired or hurt, but it should not be used too often. Save this method for emergencies or when you need to get a second wind. In competition, the referee will break the clinch after a few minutes. On the command "Break," you must move away from your opponent.

There are a variety of other defense techniques to move your head or body out of the range of blows. A few will be described, but a beginning boxer should not attempt these before developing speed, coordination, and timing.

Slipping, for example, is moving your head aside quickly as you see a blow coming toward you, letting

*In a clinch, hold your opponent's arms so he will be
unable to hit you.*

your opponent's fist slip over your shoulder. You do not move your body, so you must perfect your timing and judgment, avoiding the blow by pulling aside at the exact second the fist moves past.

The *rockaway* is a form of slipping used to protect yourself from straight blows. In the on-guard position, sway or lean away from a blow, shifting your weight to your back foot without losing your balance.

Bobbing and weaving is just what the term says. Bob the head and weave the body in and out and around to avoid a straight blow to the head. You slip and slide and duck, becoming a moving target, which is hard to hit.

"Rolling with the punches" is a phrase often used in everyday conversation. When you box, *rolling* means accepting or taking the blow as you move with it. A boxer moves backward with straight blows and to either side with hooks. If you move in the same direction that a blow is traveling, the punch may not hit you or it will have less force if it does. This sounds easy, but you have to roll at the same time the punch is thrown and know how the blow will travel. Again, it takes practice and a sense of timing, which comes with experience in the ring.

Sidestepping is a defense technique for moving quickly out of range as an opponent delivers blows. It requires skill to shift your weight and change your feet without losing your balance. It is the type of defense you would use on an opponent who "bores in" on you.

Some boxing coaches call *counter-punching* a form of defense, while others refer to this technique as an offensive one. Counter-punching is returning a punch

To slip a punch, move your head aside as you see a blow coming and let your opponent's fist slip over your shoulder.

or combination of blows after an opponent's attack. To many professionals and trainers in the game, it is the art of taking advantage of openings created by an opponent.

For example, your opponent might throw a left jab. You could catch the blow on your right glove, then with his chin unprotected, you could step left and deliver a left to that open target. All of this action takes place in a matter of seconds.

There are many different ways to counterattack. To be effective in this technique, you must put together blocking, parrying, ducking, slipping, and other defensive measures, as well as sharp, straight blows and precise hooks and uppercuts. Obviously, this requires exact judgment, timing, and control. You cannot perfect this skill overnight or even in a few weeks. But you can begin to develop a variety of counterattacks in sparring practice as you learn the art of boxing. It is an important part of the offensive and defensive tactics used in the game.

After you master some of the basic methods of defense, you will begin to put together your own moves. Many famous boxers developed their own style of defense, such as the "peek-a-boo" used by heavyweight champion Floyd Patterson during his days in the ring. This term described the way Patterson kept both hands level in front of and just to the side of his head, as if he were peeking between his raised gloves at his opponent. In this way, he used his gloves to ward off blows thrown at his head, while his elbows protected him from body punches.

Another champion, light heavyweight Archie

Moore, dropped into a crouch and raised both arms in a cross-cross fashion in front of his face, the elbows pointing out. He looked as though he were going into a kind of shell. In fact, by crouching he could protect his midsection; his gloves, arms, shoulders, and even the top of his head formed a protective shell that few opponents could break through.

In recent years, Muhammad Ali's defense in heavyweight bouts was his ability to lean back and away from punches. In his famous "rope-a-dope" maneuver, he covered himself as he leaned against the ropes and let an opponent wear himself out throwing punches that were blocked by Ali's protective arms.

It would be very difficult to copy these defense tactics exactly. Many professionals have tried and failed. But you may be able to adapt some famous defense maneuvers to your own style. First, though, you must learn the basics. As you practice, you will begin to discover what your special talents for self-defense are and how to develop these to your advantage.

If you concentrate on defense as much as offense, you will have a much better chance to win competitions. You may never receive a lot of credit for your defense tactics, because these are seldom as dramatic as blows that score points. Yet, you will emerge from the ring with fewer injuries and be well on your way to becoming an expert at the game.

6
Rules of the Game

When you go into the ring to compete against another amateur boxer, the contest will probably be conducted under the rules spelled out by the Amateur Athletic Union. Most A.A.U. rules are the same as the International Boxing Rules used for Olympic bouts and other contests in which boxers from different countries compete. If you go to a boxing gym, your coach will have a copy of the A.A.U. official rules. These are included in the A.A.U. Boxing Handbook, which is available from A.A.U. House, 3400 West 86th Street, Indianapolis, Indiana 46268 for a small cost.

You won't need to learn every technical regulation before you compete, but you should have a basic understanding of the rules of the game. As mentioned earlier, glove size and weight are regulated for competitions sanctioned or approved by A.A.U. Also hands must be wrapped with surgical-gauze bandages, using no more than one roll of gauze for each hand. Extra bandaging or tape cannot be used to create a heavy layer of padding for the knuckles.

You must dress according to rules, also. In amateur matches, each contestant must wear a sleeveless shirt and boxing trunks that reach at least halfway down the thigh. You are required to wear boxing shoes or boots without heels or spikes, a foul-proof protection cup, and a mouthpiece. Headgear may be worn, but it is not an A.A.U. requirement unless a district office establishes a rule for competition headgear. Then all boxers competing in that district must abide by the rule.

When you enter a competition, you are placed within a certain class and division. This means you are matched according to experience, age, and weight. If, for example, you have never entered a competition sanctioned by A.A.U., you would be in the *sub-novice* class. The *novice* classification is for boxers with only a few contests to their credit. The *open* class is for boxers who have been semifinalists or have won championships in district, state, and national tournaments.

In some tournaments, sub-novice boxers are divided according to age with a junior division for 10- to 11-year-olds, an intermediate division for 12- to 13-year-olds, and a senior division for 14- to 15-year-olds. In any division or class, all amateurs compete within a weight division also. For *championship* bouts, governed by A.A.U. rules, these weights are labeled:

Light Flyweight	106 pounds
Flyweight	112 pounds
Bantamweight	119 pounds
Featherweight	125 pounds
Lightweight	132 pounds
Junior Welterweight	139 pounds
Welterweight	147 pounds
Junior Middleweight	156 pounds
Middleweight	165 pounds
Light Heavyweight	178 pounds
Heavyweight	over 178 pounds

If you enter an A.A.U. championship contest in one of the weight divisions, you cannot be over the maximum weight listed for that division, but you are allowed to weigh a few pounds less. In other words, if you enter as a flyweight, you cannot weigh over 112 pounds, but you must weigh over 106 pounds, which is the limit for the first weight division.

Some young boxers compete in tournaments with weight divisions under 106 pounds. These divisions are usually determined at the time of an individual competition.

To compete in a tournament, you must *weigh in*— have your weight checked by an official weigher on the type of scale used in a medical office. The weighing-in takes place within five hours of a tournament. Then a coach or trainer will draw a number to determine the bout and with whom you will compete.

Most beginning boxers compete in two one-minute rounds, with a minute rest period between. Older, more experienced boxers often compete in three two-minute rounds, with a minute rest between each round. In district and national championship tournaments and international contests, there are three rounds of three minutes each.

Once the bout begins, you will be awarded points for each round that you box. At least three judges, sitting at tables below and on different sides of the ring, mark the points on individual score cards. The winner of any round receives 20 points for the round, while the loser receives a score ranging from 19 to a low of 14. However, if a boxer receives a score of 14, the bout should be stopped, since the contestants are too unevenly matched.

The winning points are usually awarded to the boxer who lands the most direct blows without fouling. At the end of a bout, the referee collects the score cards and hands them to an announcer who names the winner. At most contests, the announcement is made over a public-address system so that spectators can hear the results.

You can win a bout by a knockout, which means your opponent is knocked down and is unable to box after the referee counts to ten. In amateur bouts, if your opponent can continue the match after the count of eight, you will get credit for an effective blow, but you won't receive extra points for the knockdown.

You can also win a bout by retirement. This means if your opponent (or his coach) calls off the bout because of an injury or other cause, you are declared the winner. A referee may stop a contest, too. If your opponent is unable to defend himself properly, the referee will stop the fight and name you the winner.

Hitting an opponent while he's down is a foul.

If you butt an opponent like this, you are fouling.

Hitting below the belt is a foul.

During a boxing match, a referee will constantly check for fouls. The referee can either caution you without stopping the bout or issue a warning not to foul. But to warn you, the referee must stop the contest and demonstrate the foul for the judges. If you receive three warnings in a bout, you are automatically disqualified and your opponent becomes the winner. Four different fouls are demonstrated in the photos.

Other types of fouls include offensive language, locking an opponent's arm or head, wrestling, and intentionally falling down to avoid a blow. A complete list of fouls is often posted in a boxing gym, and an illustration of them appears in the A.A.U. Boxing Handbook.

The rules also cover sportsmanship in the ring. Since the game of boxing is intended to be friendly rivalry, not a "fight to the finish," you shake hands with your opponent at the beginning and end of a match. Each of you is assigned a corner, labeled "red" or "blue" and directly opposite one another in the ring. You must both go to your respective corners at the end of every round. If you knock your opponent down, you must go to a neutral corner until the referee gives the command "Box."

The referee is in charge of the entire boxing bout inside the ring. Before a boxing match begins, the referee will check to see that you and your opponent are wearing the proper protective gear and will caution you both to fight cleanly and fairly.

You will begin and end a round when you hear the sound of a gong or bell. But during the bout, the ref-

If you hit an opponent with an elbow, you are committing a foul.

eree gives the commands "Box," "Break," or "Stop." If the referee has ordered you to stop, you do not begin to box again until the referee commands "Box." The command "Break" is used when you are in a clinch. Each boxer must then step back before continuing to box. If you do not step back, the referee can call a foul or disqualify you.

A referee is required to perform many other duties in the ring, but the most important function of any amateur referee is to prevent one boxer from taking unfair advantage of another. If you are hurt in the ring, the referee will decide whether you can continue. If there is any doubt, a doctor (who must be in attendance at an amateur bout) will examine you and make the decision.

Sometimes a referee is criticized for being too strict—not allowing boxers to "mix it up" for exciting action. But a referee is responsible for the safety of contestants in the ring and must watch for any actions that will endanger boxers. By constantly checking to see that contestants follow the rules, a referee insures that boxing is a game of skills, not a show of brute force or a street fight brought indoors.

7
Treating Injuries and Fears

Anyone who is involved in sports, particularly contact sports, is bound to suffer an injury. In amateur boxing, the injuries can be kept to a minimum if you are in good condition. This cannot be stressed enough. If your body is in condition to accept blows, and if you learn to defend yourself properly, your chances of serious injury are very slight. Also, you should go to a gym where coaches and trainers provide strict supervision and emphasize safety. If this is not the case, find another gym and/or coach. When you enter a competition, you should be examined by a physician, and a doctor should be in attendance at the tournament or boxing show.

Even with all the safety precautions, you should know what kind of injuries might occur and what type of treatment to expect. During a bout, the second and an assistant will be in your corner. They are the coach and helper who will be guiding and instructing you. They also help you to relax after a round, dry you off with a towel, provide water to rinse your mouth, and administer minor first aid if necessary.

The seconds usually keep chopped ice or ice water on hand to stimulate circulation. However, any other type of stimulant between rounds can be dangerous. If a boxer is outclassed and becomes tired, confused, and uncoordinated, these are natural signs that he needs protection. The referee can then stop the bout before the weaker boxer is seriously injured. With stimulants, a boxer might keep going in spite of injuries that could cause permanent damage.

Cuts over the eye, on the nose, on the cheekbone and lip are very common in boxing. Usually the cuts bleed easily, but there is no need to panic, since there is little danger from the loss of blood. Such cuts are more of an annoyance than anything else. They prevent the boxer from doing his best job.

If there is bleeding over the eye or puffiness under the eye, this hampers vision. A coach may use a sterile pad and gentle pressure on the cut. Adrenalin hydrochloride 1/1000 solution is often used, too. This chemical solution looks like water and has no odor. It is applied on a sterile pad or swab and placed on a cut for a few seconds. It is painless, and it quickly shrinks or draws blood vessels together so that bleeding stops. The solution won't damage the skin, and it won't cause any harm if a few drops get into the eye.

A nosebleed is also common. Often, this can be stopped with the adrenalin solution on swabs or with a piece of ice under the lip. Sometimes pinching the nostrils together will help stop the bleeding. You should never blow your nose if it is bleeding.

Once in a while, a boxer might suffer a broken nose. It will swell, and usually there is continued bleeding and soreness. The injury should be checked by a nose specialist so that no permanent damage results.

Most boxers expect to have a black eye. If you are hit on the eye, you can treat the injury yourself by applying ice packs for a half hour immediately afterward. Continue with warm gentle massages later that day and several times during the next. A thumb in the eye can be treated with cold packs.

A cauliflower ear, which is a distortion of the external ear, used to be the badge of a fighter, but there is no reason this kind of permanent injury should happen, today. If there is bleeding because of a blow to the ear, cold packs can be applied. If blood continues to collect and form a tumor, this can be treated safely and quickly by a doctor. Neglecting the tumor will cause the distortion.

Bruises and abrasions are other common injuries in boxing. Cleanse the affected areas thoroughly with soap and water, and antiseptic.

You should be able to prevent a chipped or broken tooth or a fractured jaw by using a good mouthpiece. As was mentioned, this is a required piece of equipment in boxing competitions sanctioned by A.A.U. In other boxing shows and in sparring practice, be sure to use the mouthpiece for protection.

If you suspect any kind of fracture of the jaw or other bone area, go to a physician for an X-ray. A fracture is a break in a bone, and one of the symptoms of this type of injury is a sharp pain with the least movement of the area. You might also feel a roughness at the point of fracture.

What happens if you get hit in the midsection? If you are too relaxed, such a blow could cause you to lose your breath and collapse. This is why you condition your abdominal muscles, keeping them taut and firm. A solar plexus blow can sometimes result in nausea and dizziness, but smelling salts will help a boxer revive.

When a boxer is knocked out, the recommended procedure is to let him lie quietly until he regains consciousness and can walk away without help. Then cold water can be applied to his face. Other stimulants should not be used.

Sometimes beginning boxers are so afraid of being hit, knocked out, or injured that they become immobilized. They are reluctant to go into the ring to box. Nobody wants to get hurt, and there is nothing wrong with being afraid. Everyone who has ever boxed has known fear before meeting his opponent. The point is to make fear work for you. Fear is healthy if it keeps you alert.

You can fight negative fears by being physically and mentally ready when you go into the ring. If you have been matched equally with sparring partners during practice sessions, you will have learned that you can deliver as well as take punches. This knowledge should be part of your positive mental approach. Also, if you have maintained a good conditioning program, you know you are strong enough to withstand blows that come your way.

Another factor to keep in mind is that your opponent is just as fearful as you are. This may not show because some boxers are adept at hiding their fears. One might dance around the ring, acting as though he is completely free of worries. Another might glare at you. Still another might brag and strut outside the ring to build a reputation for being a tough guy. Some boxers can even make you believe they are fearless by being very calm, quiet and meditative. As you observe other boxers' "fronts" or methods used to mask fear, you may begin to develop your own act.

Once a match begins, though, all acting must be put aside. Then there is no time to be afraid. You have to think about what you are going to do, and how to do it. With a good fight plan, a positive attitude, and a coach in your corner to urge you on, you will soon forget about fear and do your job. The more successful you are at that job, the more your confidence will build. This doesn't mean that you will eventually lose all your fears. You won't, and you shouldn't. You will simply be using your healthy fear to your own advantage.

8

Taking Charge in the Ring

Some boxers call it "ring strategy." Others say it is "ring generalship." Both terms mean keeping a plan of action in your mind and taking charge in the ring during a bout.

There are as many different ways to plan a fight as there are fighters, but generally you should have a strategy or game plan that takes advantage of your opponent's weaknesses and prevents a successful attack against you. That is not as simple as it appears, so here are some tips for putting a specific plan together.

Be in good physical condition and maintain a positive attitude. You have read that advice before. But no fight plan, no clever combinations, no fancy footwork or dazzling defenses can succeed for any length of time if you are not in shape—mentally and physically.

Study your opponent. In most amateur contests you

will know who the boxers are in your weight class and who has been matched against you. Think about the person you are going to box. Ask questions about him. Find out what kind of boxer he is. Does he have a long reach? How does your reach compare—are your arms shorter or longer? Does he crowd or stalk an opponent? Is he a slugger, pounding away without much variation in his punches? Does he have the stamina to last three rounds? What can you do to tire him or outwit him?

Watch how your opponent is affected by a fight. After a bout begins, take note of your opponent's condition. If he is breathing heavily or shows other signs of getting tired, try to gain a psychological edge by masking your own tiredness. Appear energetic, particularly between rounds. Your opponent could become even more tired simply by believing that you have more energy than he has.

During a bout try to be relaxed while keeping alert. In other words, don't try so hard that you become tense, slowing down your reaction time. You might be so confused or even fearful for your first few amateur bouts that you forget everything you have been taught. That is a common condition for beginning boxers. When you feel yourself out of control, not sure what you are going to do next, try to pull yourself together by remembering that your coach is in the corner, ready to calm you. Just the thought that you have support might do the trick. If not, you will receive instructions and encouragement from a corner man between rounds.

Review the fundamentals (blows, blocks, basic posi-

At the beginning of a bout, when you are being intro-duced, and during the match, display as much confidence as possible. That should be part of your fight plan.

tion) in your mind, and be prepared to use them. During a bout, you should never let up. Keep trying and constantly look for openings to land effective blows. Even if you should get behind in points, it only takes one blow for a knockout and a win.

Don't box as your opponent expects you to box. For example, if your opponent expects you to use a hook, try another blow instead. If you become known as a slugger, don't start out that way. Lay back for a while and let your opponent come to you.

Learn the art of feinting. This one won't be easy for a beginner. Usually you need plenty of experience and practice in the ring to feint effectively. This is a method for fooling an opponent, similar to the techniques used in football or basketball when a player fakes a pass or pretends to throw a ball to a teammate but passes to another instead. In boxing, you can appear to deliver a blow or to move in a certain direction, throwing your opponent off guard—he expects one thing, but you do another.

One of the most common feints is to pretend to use a left jab to the body but hook to the head instead. Another is to fake a left jab and almost instantly shoot a straight right. Neither feint will work of course unless your opponent tries to block your pretense at a jab, thus dropping his guard and leaving an opening so that you can quickly deliver your hook or straight blow.

Sometimes you can fool an opponent by the slightest move of your shoulder, head or feet, but all types of feints have to be practiced many, many times in shadowboxing, on the heavy bag, and while sparring with a partner. If you do not feint correctly in the ring, your opponent has a chance to take advantage of the opening you leave and connect with a blow.

Don't telegraph a punch. When you are delivering blows that are part of your fight plan, try not to let your opponent know what you are going to do each time. You might give away your plan to use a left jab just by a peculiar twitch of your shoulder, a twist of your head, or even by the way you clear your throat. The secret is not to develop gestures or habitual sounds before your delivery. Use crisp, sharp blows.

Don't take your opponent lightly. You should convince yourself that you can be a winner, but do not assume that you can do this easily. Be prepared to fight three rounds if necessary. If you take your opponent for granted and drop your guard—whether literally, by dropping your arms, or mentally, by not being alert—you leave yourself open for blows that will hit their target.

Show that you are confident even when hurt and/or tired. If a blow connects, don't let your opponent know that you have been hurt. Get on your toes, move around, talk, smile, ask your opponent questions about his ability to hit—use whatever strategy you can to show that you are able to take a punch. If you are in good shape, you will quickly shake off the effects of a well-landed blow and continue with your own offense and defense.

Don't panic if you are cut. If you are bleeding, whether from the nose or from a cut on the face, you might have to change your strategy and method of fighting. Remember to keep your hands up with your chin tucked down to protect the side that has been cut.

You might have to devise ways to keep your opponent away from you until the round is over. At the same time, you will have to be on the alert for openings so that you can take the offense, if and when the opportunity presents itself. There will be a lot of things to keep in mind all at once. Be calm, cool, and patient until your corner man can check out the cut, stop the bleeding and determine how seriously you have been injured.

If you are knocked down, relax and take the mandatory eight count. You might get up on your feet and be ready to box well before a count is over, but the rules require that the referee count to eight before allowing a boxer to continue to fight. Use those seconds to breathe deeply and rest, and to think carefully about what you are going to do next.

Be aware of the time left in a bout. If you realize that there are only a few seconds to the end of a match, you can use your reserve to "burn" your opponent. In other words, you can let loose with everything you've got, using a flurry of punches or combinations. Your opponent would not expect such a tactic, and it could result in a win for you.

Learn what tactics are effective against different types of boxers. In amateur competitions your opponent will always be the same or within a few pounds of your weight, but he might not be the same size, and he may have a style quite different from yours. Here are a few general guidelines for the game plans to use against six different opponents:

1. *The tall boxer.* Set the pace with a boxer taller than yourself. Be constantly on the alert and keep

moving. Press forward and get inside a tall boxer's longer arms. Keep your opponent off balance with infighting techniques—using short range blows such as uppercuts.

2. *The southpaw.* A left-handed boxer often uses hooks and uppercuts. Don't lead. Let him come to you. Circle left, away from the southpaw's left hook, and use your right to the head or body. You should also learn to use a left hook against a southpaw, since delivering straight rights leaves you open for your opponent's left to the body.

3. *The slugger.* A fighter who uses this style of boxing often gets set and pounds away, or simply moves straight in with a constant barrage of punches. Your strategy should be to keep moving and attack suddenly with jabs and straight rights. Sidestep or tie him up with a clinch. Repeat this kind of procedure so you won't get cut or worn out.

4. *The croucher.* A short boxer often fights from a crouched position because it makes his body an even smaller target and he can get in close for infighting, pounding away with body punches. Sidestep a croucher and use a one-two combination. If you miss your blows, use a clinch to stop the croucher from getting inside.

5. *The jabber.* If your opponent has perfected the left jab, flicking it out constantly as he dances out of reach ("stick and move" is the phrase you often hear from trainers urging such a boxer on), you will have to keep low and slip the blows. Make him lead, and force the jab so you can time it and get your right over the top of your opponent's left hand.

6. *The rusher.* This boxer is the type who has not developed many skills and rushes in or presses close. If an opponent rushes you, sidestep and counter with a blow. You might also use a one-two, jabbing with a left to the chin and following with a straight right. When you are in close, clinch with your weight on your opponent to help tire him.

As you gain more and more experience in the ring, you will develop other tactics. Every game plan will be a little different, depending on the type of boxer you have as an opponent. You may want to "cut the ring in half," which is a strategy to keep your opponent boxed in one half of the ring. You move quickly from side to side so that he cannot dance away from you and prevent you from moving in on him.

Your plan might include using a lot of body blows during a bout so that you can wear your opponent out. Maybe you will keep your opponent away from you by using a continual pattern of jabs. If you discover that your opponent has developed a powerful blow, such as a left hook, you must plan to backpedal away from it, circling left so that you won't move into it.

Whatever type of boxer you meet, you will probably have to change your plan somewhat along the way. No opponent will fight exactly as you expect, anymore than you want to box as your opponent anticipates. You can adapt your plan—with the help of a good coach—to fit a specific situation.

This doesn't mean that you have to change your style of boxing. The point is, you should plan how to use your particular methods of offense and defense in the best possible way. You should also learn how to solve problems as they come up during a bout. Don't be discouraged if you can't carry out all of your tactics immediately. Just remember to use your intelligence. That's what planning is all about. It helps you organize what you are going to do so that you can take charge in the ring.

9
Developing a Style

You will hear a lot of talk about style when you are working out in a boxing gym and advance in the sport. If you are a professional boxing fan, you know the style of a boxer is an important part of a show, and pros often become known for the blows and defense techniques they perfect.

Almost everyone has heard of Joe Louis, who was the world heavyweight champion in the late 1930s and through the 1940s. He was often called the "Brown Bomber," which described his uncomplicated style—to stay with his opponent and go after him until he could put him out of the game. Louis would plow in to force his opponent to fight. There was nothing fancy or slick about it. He simply tried to catch his opponent as quickly as possible and hit him with a punch that was "like being nailed with a crowbar," as one contender put it.

Rocky Marciano, who never lost a professional fight, was short for a heavyweight. With his reach of only 68 inches, his style consisted of slamming in to throw punches and to take them. As the name he gave himself implies, he was like a rock. He developed such power in both hands that he could knock out an opponent with either one.

"Smokin' Joe" Frazier has often been compared to Marciano for his similar style, developed partly because of being shorter than most heavyweights. He would often say before his bouts that he would be "comin' out smokin' "—which he did. His style, like Marciano's, was to get inside, smash away at his opponent's body, then go for the head. To do this, he trained himself to take blows in order to land a devastating punch of his own.

The "peek-a-boo" style of Floyd Patterson has already been described. Patterson also originated what he called a "gazelle punch," leaping in the air to hit an opponent.

If you go through a list of professional boxing champions, you can come up with a number of boxers whose unorthodox styles are better known than their actual boxing careers. The welterweight Kid Gavilan, for example, is a name immediately associated with the "bolo punch." Gavilan would wind up his right arm and throw a punch as if he were wielding a *bolo,* which is a long, heavy knife used to cut sugar cane in the Philippines.

The popular middleweight Sugar Ray Robinson, who won the world championship five times, developed his style around speed and perfect coordination, which he credited with giving him a knockout punch. He also used fancy footwork—which came from his first love, dancing—to maneuver his opponents and set them up for his powerful punch.

A style often develops because of a specific talent or ability or because of the build and size of a boxer. As a beginner, you might want to imitate the tactics or blows used by one of your favorite pros or amateur Olympic champions. You can do this up to a point, but you should spend your time perfecting your own style. If not, you might lose more bouts than you win.

When Howard Davis was an amateur contender in the 1976 Olympic contests, he tried to copy all of Muhammad Ali's famous tactics. But it didn't work, so he went back to his own way of jabbing with a snappy left hand and moving out quickly.

Some beginning boxers develop elements of a style very early in their training. Let's say that you are a boxer who has tried over and over again to fight from the classic on-guard position, with your right hand up protecting your chin. Your trainer or coach constantly urges you to keep your hand in that position, but you find you cannot deliver a blow or you are always uncomfortable. Maybe you will have to keep your hands just below the classic position. If you are able to do this, and block a punch and throw it at the same time, then that element of your style works. So you keep it and try to improve on it.

You can pick up different elements for your own brand of boxing as you move along in acquiring skills. If you start out in an unorthodox manner, you might have to change your style later in order to become an effective boxer. After you learn the fundamentals, you can add or change the basics to fit your particular abilities.

An example of this is developing a manner of avoiding punches. First you learn to step back or to bob and weave; then you might use your own swing-and-sway movements that suit you and at the same time are an effective guard.

Perhaps you will learn to deliver blows in a flat-footed manner, rather than shifting your weight to the ball of the foot. You could be taught a jabbing style, but find later on that you want to add other combinations and flurries to develop tactics that are more complex and confusing to an opponent.

The more you perfect certain techniques, the more you are likely to add flourishes such as dance steps, walk-aways, or even gestures to urge your opponent on. You should not only feel comfortable with your methods, your tactics should also help you win in competition. Otherwise, stick with the basics and a more orthodox style of boxing.

Often, a style reflects a boxer's personality, culture, and certain natural abilities. The straight-on, almost robot style of some European boxers, for example, comes in part from their disciplined training and conditioning, which follows traditional methods. On the other hand, many American boxers have had less formal training and are free to improvise. They might use rhythmic movements and unusual ways of delivering blows. Some develop a "hungry style," grinding on, mixing it up to take dozens of blows just to land that knockout punch.

There is just as much diversity in the styles of boxers in the amateur ranks as there is in the professional field, which means that a beginning boxer should have a lot of sparring practice before going into competition. You should spar with partners who box differently than you do so that you can gain experience using your offensive and defensive tactics against various styles. Too often, an amateur who practices only at home, training on a heavy bag, shadowboxing and getting into good physical condition, thinks this is all it takes to get ready for a contest.

All of the home training is great, but a heavy bag will not hit back, and a boxer cannot duck a blow from a shadow. You absolutely have to have sparring practice in order to develop the coordination, split-second timing, and reflexes you will need when you box in a real bout against a live opponent.

You should spar regularly if you want to compete successfully as a boxer. A boxing gym is the best place to find sparring partners who match your age and weight and have similar skills. It is also the place to find qualified coaches who can watch your moves and blows, pointing out ways to improve.

In sparring practice, you learn to connect with a blow against a moving target. You learn to slip a punch or sidestep as your partner delivers blows. Sparring helps you develop stamina as you keep up with your partner or try to outmaneuver him. Finally, as you practice in a sparring session, you find your own way of boxing that is natural and comfortable, but controlled and well-planned. It is an essential part of developing your own style.

10
Preparing for Competition

All of your conditioning, training, and practice would mean little if you could not compete. In amateur boxing, a variety of contests take place across the country year round. Boxing clubs in one area of a state or in a big city compete with each other on a regular basis. So do boxing teams that are part of programs sponsored by the Police Athletic League (P.A.L.), park districts, the Y's, and other youth groups.

If you want to compete in a major tournament such as Golden Gloves or Junior Olympics—which is a series of competitions—you should plan your training routine carefully. Your first step is to make sure you are registered with A.A.U. Most amateur boxing contests and all major tournaments for amateur boxers are conducted under A.A.U. supervision, so all participants must be A.A.U. members. A boxing coach, school gym teacher or youth leader can help you apply for annual membership.

The next step is to check your calendar. If you have been training on a regular basis for most of the year, you need a few weeks off for R & R—rest and relaxation. This allows time for normal growth. Sometimes young, highly disciplined athletes actually add inches to their height when they relax their rigid training. Then, six weeks before a tournament, you can start concentrated efforts to put yourself in top physical and mental condition.

Get back into your routine slowly. At first, you will have to get the kinks out with a few of the calisthenics described in Chapter 2 and by running 8-12 laps around a quarter-mile track on an athletic field (or 2-3 miles of running). Use this routine for two evenings a week for the first two weeks—or work out in the morning if this is a better time of day for you.

During the third week before a tournament, start shadowboxing again and work out on the heavy bag, along with the rope-skipping, calisthenics, and running. Also, you should be in the ring for sparring practice. Two or three evenings is enough time to allot during this period of training.

About this time, your coach will have to determine your fighting weight. Maybe you have previously been boxing in the 112-pound class, but because you grew several inches and gained during your R & R, you are now up to 130 pounds. You and your coach will have to decide whether it is wise for you to box as a bantamweight (119 pounds) or as a featherweight (125 pounds). If a lot of your extra weight is due to inactivity and improper diet, your coach might decide that you will quickly shed the pounds and should fight as a bantamweight. There are other considerations, too, such as the age and experience of most contenders in a certain class and how well you fit into it—whether you will be able to compete on an equal basis.

Once you have established what your boxing weight should be, you can plan your diet and the rest of your pretournament conditioning to meet that goal. Your attitude will have a lot to do with how successful you are. If you take a positive approach, you are likely to achieve what you set out to do, whether in training or during a competition.

The two weeks before a tournament should be spent in concentrated efforts, four or five evenings per week and one day each weekend. You should step up your routine in the gym with all of the usual procedures, plus extra work on blows, blocks, and techniques that you need to master. If you are lucky enough to have film of some of your previous bouts, you can learn by watching your own actions and correcting improper moves or adding to the techniques you have already perfected. If you have confidence in your coach's ability to advise you, listen carefully to suggestions and try to carry them out.

You've read it before, but you must keep reminding yourself that in order to excel in amateur boxing competitions, you should be serious about your training. It won't be easy, but you can find great satisfaction in the way you respond and how you feel inside when your body is in excellent physical condition. But don't kid yourself. There will be times when you will feel lazy and will hate to continue the rigid routine you have set up. Even the boxing pros, who know they must train in order to keep fighting and earning a living, admit there are parts of the training they would like to forget.

Floyd Patterson, for example, said he sometimes had to force himself to get up early in the morning to do his roadwork. He would make excuses and tell himself that he had already worked hard in the gym and might be overtraining. He realized, though, that he was only trying to fool himself and went out to do his running.

There are times when a boxer can push himself too hard, but you will know this if your reflexes are not as sharp as they usually are, when your timing is off, and when you feel so tired that you cannot function properly.

The problem is usually the opposite however. An amateur boxer is training not for his livelihood but for a trophy and a place in the spotlight if he's a winner. Yet, most amateur boxers find that just participating in the sport is worth all the effort and sacrifices because there is a feeling of accomplishment comes when an athlete applies the skills that take so long to develop.

A few days before a tournament, you should begin to taper off in your routine. Eliminate the sparring practice so that you won't be cut or hurt in any way. Instead, do your roadwork and a few calisthenics to stay loose and agile. Also, a little practice on the heavy bag for timing is fine, but don't overdo it with a strenuous workout. Continue to think positively about

Two boxers wait for a decision from the judges after an amateur boxing contest; the referee between them will raise the hand of the winner.

After a bout, winners pose with their trophies.

your upcoming contest and practice some general safety and health rules:

1. Be sure all of your protective gear is in good condition and ready to use.

2. Maintain a well-balanced diet.

3. Watch your personal cleanliness. Make sure all of your clothing, particularly underwear and socks, are clean.

4. Get enough sleep and try to be in a meditative spirit. Stay away from people who have negative influences on you. Don't let anyone convince you that you should break from your training routine.

5. If you have any bruises or small cuts on your face from sparring practice, use the necessary healing measure to clear them up before a bout.

6. Go over a variety of fight plans in your mind so that you'll be mentally prepared to face different types of boxers in the ring.

When a bout actually begins, you should not have any food in your stomach. You can easily become nauseated if you eat just before a fight. Your precontest meal should be eaten at least four hours prior to the time you go into the ring. Then, eat no more than a small portion of lean, broiled meat or chicken or two soft-boiled eggs, dry toast, and weak tea.

Finally, as you are getting ready to enter the ring, remember that you have prepared yourself for the contest. Be confident and go out to box, giving the game the best that you have.

Glossary

A.A.U.　Initials that stand for the Amateur Athletic Union, a national organization that supervises a variety of sports, including the game of boxing.

amateur boxer　A boxer who never receives money for competing in a boxing match.

attack　Taking the lead or striking a blow before an opponent does.

backpeddle　Moving away from an opponent, backward, while facing him.

bandages　Surgical gauze used to wrap a boxer's hands.

beat to the punch　Hitting an opponent before his blow strikes.

bell   A signal for a boxing round to start and to end.

block   Using part of the body to shield against a blow.

blow   A punch with the fist.

bobbing and weaving   A swaying movement of the body as a form of defense.

body punch   A blow to the body.

break   Pulling away from a clinch.

butt   A foul, which is a hit with the head or shoulder.

button   The chin.

clinch   Locking arms with an opponent.

combination   Two or more punches delivered in a rapid pattern.

counter-punch   A blow thrown in response to an opponent's lead.

cover-up   Using both arms as a defense, covering the head and body.

crouch   Bending low to box.

crowd   Moving in close to an opponent so he has no punching room.

defense   Blocks or other movements to avoid an opponent's attack.

drop   Knocking an opponent to the floor of the ring.

ducking   A method of defense in which the boxer avoids blows by dropping the body and bending forward.

elbowing   A foul; using the elbows to hit or press against an opponent's face

feint   Faking a blow to throw an opponent off-guard.

flurry   A sudden and rapid succession of blows.

foul   An illegal blow or other infraction of the boxing rules.

Golden Gloves   A shortened term for The Golden Gloves Association of America, Inc., a national organization that sponsors major boxing tournaments for amateur boxers.

hand wraps   Cotton strips used to bandage the hands for boxing practice.

heavy bag   A large bag with filler material used in training to develop powerful blows.

heeling   A foul; hitting with the butt of the hand or inside of the glove.

hook   A blow at close range, delivered in an arc.

infighting   Fighting at close range.

jab   A straight, snappy blow.

judge   An official for a boxing bout who scores boxers and watches a bout for the purpose of judging
the winner.

kayo or K.O.   Shortened forms for knockout.

knockdown   Knocking an opponent to the floor
or helpless against the ropes; a referee determines
if a boxer is "down" in a bout.

low blow   A punch below the belt line, which is a
foul.

medicine ball   A heavy ball used to strengthen a
boxer's stomach muscles during training.

mixing it up   Two boxers throwing punches,
creating excitement and action in the ring.

mouthpiece   Protective covering for the teeth.

neutral corner   Corners of the ring not used by
boxers between rounds of a bout.

Olympic games   Athletic contests held once
every four years in a different country. A.A.U.
Junior Olympics, a national program to encour-
age and promote athletics and a variety of sports
in the United States, including competition in
amateur boxing.

outbox   Boxing much better than an opponent.

outpoint   Earn more points than an opponent and
gain the decision from the judges as the winner of
a bout.

professional boxer   A person who earns money from boxing.

right cross   A blow with the right hand that crosses from right to left.

rolling   A form of defense, moving with an opponent's blow.

round   A time period in a boxing bout.

second   A coach or trainer in a boxer's corner during a contest.

shadowboxing   Practicing blows against an imaginary partner.

sparring   Boxing with a partner as practice in a training session.

stance   A way of standing and a position of the body in boxing (and other sports).

stand-up boxer   One who boxes in an orthodox position, that is, in the basic stance.

technical knockout or **T.K.O.**   When a match is stopped by the referee because of an injury or to prevent a weaker boxer from taking too much punishment.

telegraph a punch   Letting an opponent know, with unintentional signs, what blow is going to be delivered.

tie up   Clinch.

wind sprint   A short run at top speed.

Index

Queensberry rules, xiv

R & R, 95
Randolph, Leo, x
referee, 72, 74
retirement, 68
right to the body, 46
ring strategy, 80
roadwork, 16, 17
Robinson, "Sugar" Ray, 90
rockaway, 61
rolling, 61
Rome, xiii
round-house blow, 54-5
rounds, 67-8
rusher, 87

shadow boxing, 10, 41, 47-9,
    83, 93, 95
shuffling, 33
sidestepping, 61, 86

skip rope, 10
slipping, 59
slugger, 86
southpaw, 86
sparring, 41, 49, 83, 93, 97
Spinks, Leon, x
    Michael, x
stance, 26-7
stimulants, 76
straight right, 41, 83, 86
sub-novice, 66

Tunney, Gene, xiv, 19

uppercut, 47

weigh-in, 67
weight divisions, 67
weight lifters, 17
wind sprint, 17
wrestlers, 17